the **REALLY** funny

KNOCK!
KNOCK!

joke book for kids

Mickey MacIntyre

The Really Funny...
KNOCK! KNOCK! Joke Book For Kids.
Over 150 side-splitting, rib-tickling KNOCK!
KNOCK! Jokes PLUS Top 10 Tips For Telling The
Best Jokes.

Mickey MacIntyre

ISBN 978-1-909855-25-0

Contents

the REALLY funny....

Top Ten Tips For Telling Jokes

Practice, Practice, Practice!

Know your joke. Ok so it's only a short KNOCK KNOCK joke, but mess it up and no one will be laughing. Make sure you know your joke 'off by heart' and practice it in front of a mirror. Learning your lines means you can concentrate on 'telling' the joke instead of just reading it.

Know when to be quiet! Don't start explaining the joke the second you have told it. Let your audience work it out for a few seconds and they will laugh when they 'get' it.

Think about the best time to tell a joke. Telling a joke about Santa Claus in August won't get many laughs but if you're sitting at the dinner table with your family this kind of joke would fit well:

KNOCK! KNOCK! joke book for kids

Knock, knock!
Who's there?
Pudding!
Pudding who?
Pudding your shoes on before your trousers is not a good idea.

Don't announce you are about to tell a joke. Your audience is more likely to find a joke funny if they don't have a big announcement that they are about to hear something 'REALLY FUNNY'.

Don't tell everyone how funny your joke is before you tell it. It makes your audience expect too much.

Don't laugh at your own jokes until your audience has laughed. Give your audience time to 'get' the joke. Most of the best joke tellers tell their jokes with a 'straight' face.

the **REALLY** funny....

Choose your moment. There are bad times to tell a joke. For example if someone is really busy or sick, sad or has hurt themselves. Pick a time when everyone is in a good mood and wants to have some fun.

Take your time. Don't rush. Speeding through words too quickly will make it difficult to understand and if you have to repeat a joke, it's not as funny.

Speak clearly and make sure you 'get' the joke before you tell it. Think about the way the punch line should sound and practice it. If you think it's funny someone else will too!

Study your favourite comedians or anyone else you see on TV or youtube. Watch how they 'work'

the audience, how they deliver their punch lines, what they do with their hands. Learn from the professionals!!

We hope you enjoy reading and telling our 'KNOCK KNOCK!' jokes and hopefully are inspired to write a few of your own.

Enjoy!

.....now for the **REALLY** funny KNOCK! KNOCK! jokes....

KNOCK! KNOCK! joke book for kids

Knock, knock!
Who's there?
Duck.
Duck who?
JUST DUCK! They're throwing things at us!

Knock, knock!
Who's there?
Canoe.
Canoe who?
Canoe help me with my homework?

Knock, knock!
Who's there?
Warren.
Warren who?
Warren you in this same class last year?

the **REALLY** funny....

Knock, knock!
Who's there?
Tamara.
Tamara who?
Tamara is another school day. Yuk!

Knock, knock!
Who's There?
Reed.
Reed who?
Reed between the lines and you'll work it out!

Knock, knock!
Who's there?
Kermit.
Kermit who?
Ker-mit a crime and you'll go to jail!

Knock, knock!
Who's there?
Alison!
Alison who?
Alice-in Wonderland!

Knock, knock!
Who's there?
Kay.
Kay who?
Kay sera sera!

Knock, knock!
Who's there?
Mary Lee.
Mary Lee who?
Mary-Lee, Mary-Lee, life is but a dream.
Row, row, row your boat....

the REALLY funny....

Knock, knock!
Who's there?
Dawn.
Dawn who?
Dawn do anything that I wouldn't do!

Knock, knock!
Who's there?
B-2.
B-2 who?
B-2 school on time or you'll get detention!

Knock, knock!
Who's there?
Toby.
Toby who?
Toby or not to be, that is the question!

Knock, knock!
Who's there?
Wendy.
Wendy who?
Wen-dy red red robbin goes bob bob bobbin along!

Knock, knock!
Who's there?
Oddley hee.
Oddley hee who?
Wow. I didn't know you could yodel!

Knock, knock!
Who's There?
Rita.
Rita who?

Rita book, you might learn something!

Knock, knock!
Who's there?
Justin.
Justin who?
Justin time, you were nearly late!

Knock, knock!
Who's there?
Brendan.
Brendan who?
Bren-dan ear to what I am going to tell you!

Knock, knock!
Who's there?
Nadia.
Nadia who?
Nadia you head if you understand the joke!

Knock, knock!
Who's there?
To.
To who?
To whom.... Not to who!

Knock, knock!
Who's there?
Abba.
Abba who?
Abb-out turn. Quick march, quick march!

Knock, knock!
Who's there?
Barbara.
Barbara who?
Bar-bar black sheep, have you any wool?

the **REALLY** funny....

Knock, knock!
Who's there?
Adda.
Adda who?
A diamond is forever!

Knock, knock!
Who's there?
Abby.
Abby who?
Abby birthday to you!

Knock, knock!
Who's there?
Arge and Tina.
Arge and Tina who?
"Don't cry for me, Arge and Tina"!

Knock, knock!
Who's There?
Rocky.
Rocky who?
Rocky bye baby on the tree top...

Knock, knock!
Who's There?
Radio.
Radio who?
Rad-io not, here I come!

Knock, knock!
Who's there?
Joo.
Joo who?
Joo-who lets the dogs out?

the **REALLY** funny....

Knock, knock!
Who's there?
Izzy.
Izzy who?
Izzy come, Izzy go!

Knock, knock!
Who's there?
Mice.
Mice who?
Mice to meet you!

Knock, knock!
Who's there?
How low.
How low who?
How low can you go?

Knock, knock!
Who's there?
Perry.
Perry who?
Perry well, thank you. How are you?

Knock, knock!
Who's there?
Hello.
Hello who?
Hello..... and goodbye. I'm tired of waiting!

Knock, knock!
Who's there?
Peas.
Peas who?
Peas to meet you!

the **REALLY** funny....

Knock, knock!
Who's there?
Hawaii.
Hawaii who?
I'm fine, Hawaii you?

Knock, knock!
Who's there?
Egg.
Egg who?
Egg-cited to meet you so open the door!

Knock, knock!
Who's there?
You.
You who?
Yoo-hoo, I'm over here!

Knock, knock!
Who's there?
Agatha.
Agatha who?
Agatha headache. Do you have any medicine?

Knock, knock!
Who's there?
Aida!
Aida who?
I Aida lot of sweets and now I've got tummy-ache!

Knock, knock!
Who's there?
Goat.
Goat who?
Goat to the door and find out!

the **REALLY** funny....

Knock, knock!
Who's there?
Berry.
Berry who ?
Berry glad to meet you. How do you do?

Knock, knock!
Who's there?
Pig.
Pig who?
Pig me up at two o'clock and don't be late!

Knock, knock!
Who's there?
Gorilla.
Gorilla who?
Gorilla me a cheese burger, I'm hungry!

Knock, knock!
Who's there?
Abe.
Abe who?
Abe C D E F G H...!

Knock, knock!
Who's there?
Dogs.
Dogs who?
Dogs don't hoot, but owls do!

Knock, knock!
Who's there?
Lion.
Lion who?
Lion in your bed all day is lazy so get up!

the REALLY funny....

Knock, knock!
Who's there?
Cook.
Cook who?
Why are you calling me a CUCKOO?

Knock, knock!
Who's there?
Oink oink.
Oink oink who?
Make up your mind,. Are you a pig or an owl?

Knock, knock!
Who's there?
Cows go.
Cows go who?
No they don't! Cows go moooooo!

Knock, knock!
Who's There?
Amos.
Amos who?
A mosquito bit me and it's really itchy now!

Knock, knock!
Who's there?
Who...
Who who?
Are you pretending to be an owl or something?

Knock, knock!
Who's there?
Razor.
Razor who?
Raz-or hands up or I'll shoot!

the **REALLY** funny....

Knock, knock!
Who's there?
Ear.
Ear who?
Ear you are, I've been looking for you for ages!

Knock, knock!
Who's there?
Omar.
Omar who?
Om-ar goodness! I've lost my key and I'm locked out.

Knock, knock!
Who's there?
Nobel.
Nobel who?
No-bell so I'm knocking instead!

Knock, knock!
Who's there?
Eskimo!
Eskimo who?
Eskimo questions and I'll tell you no lies!

Knock, knock!
Who's there?
Royal.
Royal who?
Roy-al give you a lift if you ask him nicely!

Knock, knock!
Who's there?
Dozen!
Dozen who?
Dozen anybody know who I am anymore?

Knock, knock!
Who's there?
Dragon.
Dragon who?
Dragon my feet all the way to school will make me late again!

Knock, knock!
Who's there?
Wicked.
Wicked who?
Wi-cked make a great team if you just open the door and let me in!

Knock, knock!
Who's there?
July.
July who?
Ju-ly or do you always tell the truth?

Knock, knock!!
Who's there?
Design.
Design who?
De-sign said 'Keep Out' but can I come in?

Knock, knock!
Who's there?
I'm shad.
I'm shad who?
I'm shad to see you go, so please stay!

Knock, knock!
Who's there?
Ida Kline.
Ida Kline who?
I-dakline to answer your questions so stop asking me!

Knock, knock!
Who's there?
Dummy.
Dummy who?
Du-mmy a favour and open the door!

Knock, knock!
Who's there?
Howl.
Howl who?
Ho-wl you know unless you open the door?

Knock, knock!
Who's there?
Wire.
Wire who?
Wi-re you asking, don't you know me?

Knock, knock!
Who's there?
Poker.
Poker who?
Poke'er again and she'll poke you back!

Knock, knock!
Who's there?
Ivor.
Ivor who?
I-vor you let me in or I'll climb through the window and let myself in!

Knock, knock!
Who's there?
I dunn op.
I dunn op who?
Hahahaha... YOU DONE A POO!

the **REALLY** funny....

Knock, knock!
Who's there?
Witches!
Witches who?
Witch-es the way to get home? I'm lost!

Knock, knock!
Who's there?
Wooden shoe.
Wooden shoe who?
Wooden shoe like to hear another joke?

Knock, knock!
Who's There?
Romeo.
Romeo who?
Romeo-ver to the other side of the river!

Knock, knock!
Who's there?
Yula.
Yola who?
Yul-apologise for not letting me in straight away when you see who it is!

Knock, knock!
Who's there?
Liz.
Liz who?
Liz-see what you look like when you open the door!

Knock, knock!
Who's there?
Demure.
Demure who?
Demure the merrier!

the REALLY funny....

Knock, knock!
Who's there?
Sew.
Sew who?
Sew what else is happening?

Knock, knock!
Who's there?
Figs.
Figs who?
Figs the doorbell will ya, then I won't have to knock!

Knock, knock!
Who's there?
CD's.
CD's Who?
CD's hands? They're sore from all this knocking!

Knock, knock!
Who's there?
Ooze.
Ooze who?
Ooze that knocking at my door?

Knock, knock!
Who's there?
Onya.
Onya who?
Onya marks, get set, go!

Knock, knock!
Who's there?
Toodle.
Toodle who?
Toodle-oo to you, too!

the REALLY funny....

Knock, knock!
Who's there?
Oslo.
Oslo who?
Oslo down, you're going way too fast!

Knock, knock!
Who's there?
Sadie.
Sadie who?
Sadie magic words and I'll tell you!

Knock, knock!
Who's there?
A little somone.
A little someone who?
A little someone who can't reach the doorbell!

Knock, knock!
Who's there?
Sari.
Sari who?
Sari wrong number!

Knock, knock!
Who's there?
Emmett.
Emmett who?
**Emmett the front door, not
the back one!**

Knock, knock!
Who's there?
Luke.
Luke who?
Luke out, the cops are after you!

Knock, knock!
Who's there?
Nova.
Nova who?
Nova look back just keep on going straight ahead!

Knock, knock!
Who's there?
Won.
Won who?
Won for your life, here comes the monster!

Knock, knock!
Who's there?
Avenue.
Avenue who?
Avenue guessed yet? It's me!

Knock, knock!
Who's there?
Brad.
Brad who?
Brad news I'm afraid. Your doorbell is broken!

Knock, knock!
Who's there?
Turnip.
Turnip who?
Turnip the volume, and dance!

Knock, knock!
Who's there?
Owl.
Owl who?
Owl I can say is "Knock, knock"!

the REALLY funny....

Knock, knock!
Who's there?
Hatch.
Hatch who?
Bless you, but please cover your mouth when you sneeze in future!

Knock, knock!
Who's there?
Tank.
Tank Who?
You're welcome!

Knock, knock!
Who's there?
Thermos.
Thermos who?

Thermos be a better knock, knock joke than this!

Knock, knock!
Who's there?
Ahab.
Ahab who ?
Ahab to go to the toilet NOW so open the door!

Knock, knock!
Who's there?
Boo.
Boo who?
There's no need to cry, it's only a joke.

Knock, knock!
Who's there?
Champ.
Champ who?

Champ poo your hair will you. When's the last time you had a shower?

the REALLY funny....

Knock, knock!
Who's there?
Latin.
Latin who?
Latin me in would be a good way for you to find out!

Knock, knock!
Who's there?
Donna.
Donna who?
Donna come outside. It's raining!

Knock, knock!
Who's there?
Roach.
Roach who?
Roach you a letter, telling you I was coming. Didn't you get it?

Knock, knock!
Who's there?
Value.
Value who?
Value be my Valentine?

Knock, knock!
Who's there?
Toto.
Toto who?
Totolly devoted to you!

Knock, knock!
Who's there?
Keith.
Keith who?
Keith me, thweet heart!

the REALLY funny....

Knock, knock.
Who's there?
Ina.
Ina who?
Ina minute!

Knock, knock!
Who's there?
Ice cream.
Ice cream who?
Ice cream and scream until you let me in!

Knock, knock!
Who's there?
Viola.
Viola who?
Viola sudden you don't know who I am?

Knock, knock!
Who's there?
Dana.
Dana who?
Dana pretend you don't know me!

Knock, knock!
Who's there?
Dishes.
Dishes who?
Dishes getting boring! Just let me in!

Knock, knock!
Who's there?
Sweden.
Sweden who?
Sweden sour and some prawn cracker please!

Knock, knock!
Who's there?
Pudding.
Pudding who?
Pudding your shoes on before your trousers is not a good idea!

Knock, knock!
Who's there?
Oil.
Oil who?
Oil be seeing you later!

Knock, knock!
Who's there?
Noah.
Noah who?
Noah good place to eat? I'm starving.

Knock, knock!
Who's there?
Barbie.
Barbie who?
Bar-B-Q.

Knock, knock!
Who's there?
Water.
Water who?
Water you doing in my house? Get out.

Knock, knock!
Who's there?
Marsh.
Marsh who?
Marshmallow!

the **REALLY** funny....

Knock, knock!
Who's there!
Butter.
Butter who?
Butter let me in before I knock the door down!

Knock, knock!
Who's there?
Lettuce.
Lettuce who?
Lettuce in will you. We're freezing!

Knock, knock!
Who's there?
Mary.
Mary who?
Merry Christmas & a happy new year!

Knock, knock!
Who's there?
Dexter.
Dexter who?
Dexter halls with boughs of holly fa la la la la!

Knock, knock!
Who's there?
Fanta.
Fanta who?
Fanta Claus. Ho ho ho!

Knock, knock!
Who's there?
Repeat.
Repeat who?
Who Who Who!

Knock! knock!
Who's there?
Rabbit.
Rabbit who?
Rabbit up neatly, it's a present!

Knock! knock!
Who's there?
Wanda.
Wanda who?
Wanda know what you're getting for Christmas?

Knock knock!
Who's There?
Rain.
Rain who?
Rain dear, you know, Rudolph the red nosed reindeer!

Knock, knock!
Who's there?
Doughnut.
Doughnut who?
Doughnut open until Christmas Day! It's a surprise!

Knock, knock!
Who's there ?
Oakham.
Oakham who ?
Oakham all ye faithful. Joyful and triumphant!

Knock, knock!
Who's there?
Hosanna.
Hosanna who?
How's sanna claus gonna get in here. There's no chimney!

the **REALLY** funny....

Knock, knock!
Who's there?
Hanna.
Hanna who?
.... Hanna partridge in a pear tree!

Knock, knock!
Who's there?
Santa.
Santa who?
Santa Claus!

Knock, knock!
Who's there?
Bruce.
Bruce who?
I Bruce easily, so please don't hit me!

Knock, knock!
Who's there?
Sarah.
Sarah who?
Sarah doctor in the house? I'm sick!

Knock, knock!
Who's there?
Anita.
Anita who?
Anita a tissue! Ah-choo!

Knock, knock!
Who's there?
Caesar.
Caesar who?
Caesar jolly good fellow!

the **REALLY** funny....

Knock, knock!
Who's there?
Isabelle.
Isabelle who?
Isabelle the only way to get in? I keep on knocking but no ones answering!

Knock, knock!
Who's there?
Eddie.
Eddie who?
Eddie-body home?

Knock, knock!
Who's there?
Carrie.
Carrie who?
Carrie me all the way to school will ya. I'm tired!

Knock knock!
Who's there?
Rupert.
Rupert who?
Rupert your left arm in, your left arm out, in-out in-out shake it all about...

Knock, knock!
Who's There?
Rio.
Rio who?
Rio-rrange your bedroom. It's a mess!

Knock knock!
Who's there?
Howie.
Howie who?
Howie going to figure out how to open this door?

the **REALLY** funny....

Knock, knock!
Who's there?
Ike.
Ike who?
I can see you through the keyhole!

Knock, knock!
Who's there?
Thea.
Thea who?
Thea-later, alligator!

Knock, knock.
Who's there?
Elly.
Elly who?
Ellymentary, my dear Watson.

Knock, knock!
Who's there?
Phillip.
Phillip who?
Fill-up the biscuit tin, I'm starving!

Knock, knock!
Who's there?
Colleen.
Colleen who?
Colleen up your room, it's a mess!

Knock! knock!
Who's there?
Olive.
Olive who?
Olive across the road. Hello!

Knock, knock!
Who's there?
Ken.
Ken who?
Ken you tell me some good knock, knock jokes?

Knock, knock!
Who's there?
Annie.
Annie who?
Annie one you like!

Knock, knock!
Who's there?
General Lee.
General Lee who?
Generally I do not tell jokes. But this one is funny!

Knock, knock!
Who's there?
Doris.
Doris who?
Doris locked, that's why I'm knocking!

Knock, knock!
Who's there?
Alex.
Alex who?
Alex-plain later just let me in!

Knock, knock!
Who's there?
Woody.
Woody who?
Woody you want!

the REALLY funny....

Knock, knock!
Who's there?
Norway.
Norway who?
Norway am I telling you any more knock, knock jokes!

Knock, knock!
Who's there?
Francis.
Francis who?
France is a country in Europe!

Knock, knock!
Who's There?
Rome.
Rome who?
Rome is where the heart is!

Knock, knock!
Who's there?
Alaska.
Alaska who?
Alaska later, right now I'm trying to work out where she is!

Knock, knock!
Who's there?
Genoa.
Genoa who?
Genoa, cos I've never seen her before in my life!

Knock, knock!
Who's there?
Jamaica.
Jamaica who?
Jamaica her do that, or is she just mad?

Knock, knock!
Who's there?
Wiltshire.
Wiltshire who?
Wiltshire sit down and I'll tell you!

Knock, knock!
Who's there?
Eureka.
Eureka who?
Eureka something, and it really stinks!

Knock, knock!
Who's there?
Yukon.
Yukon who?
Yukon never get bored of knock knock jokes!

Knock, knock!
Who's there?
Moscow.
Moscow who?
Moscow home, it's dinnertime!

Knock, knock!
Who's there?
Osborne.
Osborne who?
Osborne today - it's my birthday!

Knock, knock!
Who's there?
Maida.
Maida who?
Maida force be with you!

the **REALLY** funny....

More REALLY Funny Joke Books

You may also enjoy **'The REALLY Funny Doctor! Doctor! Joke Book For Kids'**.

And

'The REALLY Funny LOL! Joke Book For Kids'.

Plus look out for more ***REALLY* Funny** joke books from **Mickey MacIntyre** coming soon. Just search Mickey MacIntyre on **Amazon**.

Printed in Great Britain
by Amazon